The Hummel
Birthday Book

with authentic Hummel pictures

ars edition

Believing hear, what you deserve to hear:
Your birthday as my own to me is dear.
Blest and distinguish'd days!
Which we should prize
The first, the kindest bounty of the skies.
But yours gives most; for mine did only lend
Me to the world;
Yours gave me a friend

Martial

It is lovely,
when I forget all birthdays,
including my own,
to find that somebody remembers me.

Ellen Glasgow

I don't know what you think about
anniversaries. I like them,
being always minded to drink my cup of life
to the bottom, and take my chances
of the sweets and bitter.

Thomas Huxley

Our birthdays are feathers
in the broad wing of time.

Jean Paul Richter

A good laugh is a mighty good thing,
and a rather too scarce thing;
The more's the pity.

Hermann Melville

He deserves Paradise
who makes his companions laugh.

Mohammed

You cannot harnass happiness.

Russian proverb

All to myself I think of you,
Think of the things we used to do,
Think of the things we used to say,
Think of each happy bygone day.
Sometimes I sigh, and sometimes I smile,
But I keep each olden golden while
All to myself.

Wilbur Nesbit

Guard within yourself that treasure, Kindness.
Know how to give without hesitation,
how to lose without regret,
how to acquire without meanness.
Know how to replace in your heart,
by the happiness of those you love,
the happiness that may be wanting in yourself.

George Sand

Who is the happiest of men?
He who values the merits of others
And in their pleasure takes joy,
even as though it were his own.

Johann Wolfgang von Goethe

The greater part of our happiness
or our misery depends on our dispositions
and not on our circumstances.

Martha Washington

If a man looks sharply and attentively,
he shall see Fortune;
for though she is blind,
she is not invisible.

Francis Bacon

Count your garden by the flowers
Never by the leaves that fall;
Count your days by the golden hours,
Don't remember clouds at all.
Count the nights by stars not shadows,
Count your life by smiles, not tears,
And with joy on every birthday
Count your age by friends, not years.

Anonymous

All Kings, and all their favorites,
All glory of honor, beauties, wits,
The sun itself, which makes times, as they pass,
Is elder by a year, now, than it was.

John Donne

Glories, like glowworms, afar off shine bright,
But looked to near, have neither heat nor light.

John Webster

Sits he on never so high a throne,
a man still sits on his bottom.

Michel de Montaigne

Every gift, though it be small,
is in reality great if given
with affection.

Pindar

We should give as we would receive,
cheerfully, quickly, and without hesitation;
for there is no grace in a benefit
that sticks to the fingers.

Seneca

He gives little
who gives much with a frown;
He gives much
who gives little with a smile.

The Talmud

It ain't the value of the thing,
    Ner how it's wrapped ner tied;
It's somethin' else aside from this
    That makes you glad inside.
It's knowin' that it represents
    A love both deep and true
That someone carries in his heart
    An' wants to slip to you.

Anonymous

21

Make the coming hour o'erflow with joy,
And pleasure drown the brim.

Shakespeare

The supreme happiness of life
is the conviction that we are loved.

Victor Hugo

Happiness comes not from without
but from within. It comes not from
the power of possession but from
the power of appreciation.

J. Walter Sylvester

We keep the day. With festal cheer,
With books and music, surely we
Will drink to him, whate'er he be,
And sing the songs he loved to hear.

Alfred, Lord Tennyson

A man hath no better thing under the sun
than to eat, and to drink, and to make merry.

Ecclesiastes

And frame your mind to mirth and merriment,
Which bars a thousand harms and lengthens life.

Shakespeare

Occupy thyself with pleasure daily.

Ancient Egyptian proverb

My birthday began with the water –
Birds and the birds of the winged trees
flying my name.

Dylan Thomas

Music is in all growing things;
And underneath the silky wings
    Of smallest insects there is stirred
    A pulse of air that must be heard
Earth's silence lives, and throbs, and sings.

Mary Lathrop

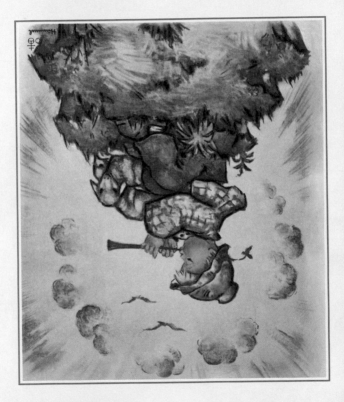

Grief can take care of itself,
but to get the full value out of joy
you must have someone to divide it with.

Mark Twain

A man that fortune's buffets and rewards,
Hast ta'en with equal thanks.

Shakespeare

Hope is itself a species of happiness,
and perhaps the chief happiness
which this world affords.

Samuel Johnson

All love is sweet,
Given or returned.
    Common as light is love,
And its familiar voice
        wearies not ever.

Percy Bysshe Shelley

Happiness makes up in height
for what it lacks in length.

Robert Frost

Love unsought is good,
but given unsought is better.

Shakespeare

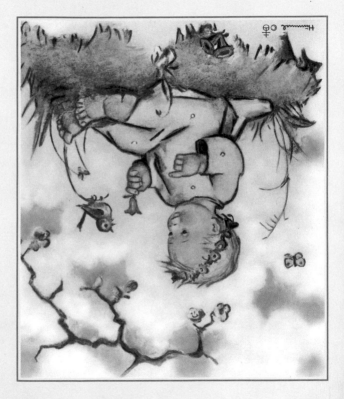

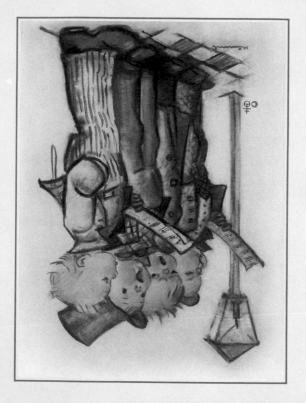

One song leads on to another,
One friend to another friend,
So I'll travel along
With a friend and a song.

Wilfred Gibson

We at Ars Edition hope this little book has brought you pleasure. The pages of this collector's edition are folded back-to-back, in a style known as Japanese binding. You may wish to collect all these beautiful Hummel books:

> The Hummel Friendship Book
> The Hummel Thank You Book
> The Hummel Get Well Book
> The Hummel Birthday Book

For the store nearest you which carries our Hummel books, please write us.

ars edition inc.

"The Original Hummel People"

70 Air Park Drive, Ronkonkoma, NY 11779

© 1983 ars edition · all rights reserved
arranged and edited by Jonathan Roth
printed in West Germany · ISBN 0-86724-054-7